LONGMAN INT1

FOR
GENERAL PSYCHOLOGY

Cheryl J. Hamel, Ph.D.
Valencia Community College
&
David L. Ryan-Jones, Ph.D.

As a user of this Longman textbook, we are pleased to offer you FREE access to our general psychology Web site, located at the following URL:

http://longman.awl.com/psychzone

Thank you for making Longman part of your learning process!

 LONGMAN

An imprint of Addison Wesley Longman. Inc.

New York • Reading, Massachusetts • Menlo Park, California • Harlow, England
Don Mills, Ontario • Sydney • Mexico City • Madrid • Amsterdam

TRADEMARK INFORMATION

Eudora is a trademark of QUALCOMM Corporation
Microsoft Internet Explorer, Windows 95 and *Internet Mail* are trademarks of
Microsoft Corporation
Netscape is a registered trademark of Netscape Communications Corporation

The authors make no guarantee of any kind with regard to these programs or the
documentation contained in this book. The authors shall not be liable for
incidental or consequential damages in connection with, or arising out of, the
furnishing of information provided in this book.

CONTENTS

PREFACE

PREFACE

The purpose of the *Longman Internet Companion for General Psychology* is to help teachers, professionals, students, and consumers take advantage of numerous psychology resources on the Internet related to major topics in general psychology. The Internet is a world-wide computer network that brings users current information from around the world almost instantaneously. Because the volume of information is so massive, a user must become savvy about finding particular information. The *Longman Internet Companion* will help you find particular information quickly because a great number of psychology-related Internet sites have been organized for you according to the major topics in the field. We have organized the sites according to topics frequently presented in a general psychology textbook and so it is easy to supplement course textbook reading and get to precise information immediately. The *Longman Internet Companion* guides you to various types of information and discussion on the Internet, and points you to Web sites that are "master sites" for general psychology. These master sites have put together in one place an extensive array of links to resources in the field of psychology, both online and offline.

Chapter 1 of this guide explains the Internet in simple terms. It includes discussion of the World Wide Web (Web), electronic mail (E-mail), mailing lists, and discussion groups. Chapter 2 presents helpful information on how to conduct research on the Web. "Surfing" the Web or using a search tool will lead you to several types of information written by a variety of sources. These types of information are explained, and the chapter ends with Internet resources you will need when writing psychology papers. Chapters 3 lists numerous Internet sites arranged by psychology topics and gives you a short description of each site. Chapter 4 is designed for the student of psychology. The Internet provides invaluable aids to learning about psychology and how to be a successful student. It can connect you to information relevant to making psychology career decisions and to other counseling and self-help resources. Student support resources such as these are given to you in this chapter.

After these chapters, you will find Appendix A which contains a glossary of frequently used terms. Finally, there is Appendix B, which refers to major Internet sites containing large numbers of resources related to general psychology. The locations of these sites are given in the Uniform Resources Locator (URL) format, and a table for each site shows you the site's resources for information pertaining to academic research and student support. Using your Web browser, you will be able to type these addresses in the "Location:" or "Go To:" box and reach them almost immediately. The *Longman Internet Companion* sometimes refers to Internet sites other than those listed in Appendix B. These sites will be accompanied by their URL address at the place they are mentioned in the text.

The guide does not cover all possible Web sites related to general psychology that are available on the Internet. The references are meant to be starting points for further exploration of Internet resources. The guide can get you started by providing examples of sites that contain some of the information you are looking for, but there are many more sites out there than those to which we refer. If your attempts to reach a site are fruitless, as sometimes happens, try again later, just in case the server was down temporarily. Web sites often have an address change, usually to provide information more efficiently, and sometimes they go out of existence. If you cannot reach a site after numerous attempts, don't despair. We have provided you with plenty of interesting places to visit on the "information highway," and with further searching, you will find many more.

CHAPTER 1
INTRODUCTION

The Internet began as a networking of a few major universities and government agencies in the U.S. who used it to communicate scientific and academic information among themselves. With the introduction of the World Wide Web and other significant advances in Internet technology, the sharing of information is now a world-wide happening. If there is a computer anywhere in the world with information available, it is now possible for any person to access it from anywhere in the world. In addition, documents can be created by inexperienced computer users so that these users can contribute to an ever-expanding database of documents on the Web. Internet users consist of computer technologists, academic communities, scientists, military and government institutions, commercial enterprises, and the general public. It is no wonder that information available on the Internet is growing daily at staggering rates and users are required to become increasingly knowledgeable about what the Net has to offer and how it functions.

WHAT IS THE INTERNET?
The Internet can be viewed as a world-wide computer network linking a vast number of smaller networks together. The Internet is composed of several different kinds of computer networks, including commercial, educational, research, and government networks, each of which may be extensive or just local. Their computers contain large amounts of information, available for free in most cases, if you can get to the information via your computer. Each of these computers is uniquely named, and the type of network to which the computer belongs is identified in the last section of the name (e.g., .com or .co for commercial, .edu or .ac for educational, .org for nonprofit organization, and .gov or .mil for government). This network of computers, once you and your computer become part of it, enables you to communicate with people around the world through a variety of methods.

Even a person lacking computer skills can take advantage of this exciting medium thanks to a distributed information system called the World Wide Web (WWW or Web). The Web gives Internet users a visually appealing interface to information in hypertext form that is called a *page*. Hypertext is simply a collection of documents that contain references to other items available to the user. This means that when a user views a Web page on the computer screen, there will be words that are highlighted and underlined, or there will be graphical icons that represent links to other objects on the Web. These objects may consist of things such as other Web pages, text, static graphics, movies, or sound clips on the same or a different computer. If your computer has the required hardware and software, you can begin to appreciate the Web's multimedia aspects.

WHAT ARE SOME OF THE INTERNET COMPONENTS?

Information on the Web can be accessed in a number of ways. To make locating objects on the Web easier, the *Uniform Resource Locator (URL)* format was developed. A URL consists of two strings of text separated by a colon. The first string specifies the method or protocol to be used to transfer the information to your computer, and the second string is the location of the information on the Web. When you select highlighted text or icons on a Web page, you are actually selecting the URL for the information that you want to find. The standard protocol for the Web is the *Hypertext Transfer Protocol (HTTP)*. The HTTP is used when Web pages are to be viewed across the Internet. Web pages are written in a format known as *Hypertext Markup Language (HTML)*. The fact that the Web uses a standard transport protocol and a standard markup language allows any computer to access the Web regardless of it's underlying architecture or operating system.

Another common transfer protocol is the *File Transfer Protocol (FTP)*. FTP was developed to allow Internet users to transport files across the Internet. Through a mechanism known as *anonymous FTP*, you can log on to a remote computer, locate publicly accessible information, and

2

download the information to your computer without a password or system name.

Just as the Web is a distributed information retrieval system, there are two other retrieval systems still in use on the Internet. These are *Gopher* and the *Wide Area Information Server (WAIS)*. These distributed information systems were developed in the early days of the Internet to provide keyword-based search capabilities for users, but they have largely been superseded by the Web itself. This is because Web pages written in HTML are inherently structured to facilitate document searching by keyword. In addition, there are now many Web applications that have other search engines built into the software which effectively eliminate the need for Gopher or WAIS.

The Internet can be used to send messages to other users independent of the structure of the Web itself. The three most common systems for communicating with other users, depending upon whether a user wants private, semiprivate or public viewing of the message, are electronic mail (E-mail), mailing lists, and newsgroups. E-mail is relatively private, and in most circumstances, only the sender and recipient view the message. E-mail is not usually sent directly to another user's computer, but to a mail server to which the user can connect. Thus, messages may not be completely private. Both the sender and the recipient must have a mail account to access E-mail.

Mailing lists are best thought of as a system to communicate with a restricted group of individuals who share a common interest (e.g., alcoholism, genetics, or psychology). Many world-wide mailing lists are handled by a mailing list server such as *LISTSERV*. Users of LISTSERV must subscribe to the mailing list of interest, and there may be very specific prerequisites for subscription. With all mailing lists, when a subscriber posts an E-mail message to the group, all individuals receive the message and may respond to the mailer alone or to the whole group.

3

The third system of communication is *USENET*, which is organized around several thousand newsgroups with a specific interest in some topic (e.g., social psychology, divorce, or hypnosis). USENET can be thought of as a discussion system which allows messages (or articles) to be posted and read by users of newsgroups. Newsgroups serve a much larger audience than mailing lists because they are not limited to subscribers only. When you post a message to a newsgroup, your message is sent to several hundred or even thousands of systems all over the world who have a connection to the network news service.

The Internet is only one of the various networks carrying USENET traffic. USENET does not use HTTP to transfer news articles, but rather a protocol called *Network News Transport Protocol (NNTP)*. Just as E-mail access requires a mail server, network news access requires a news server.

E-MAIL
Electronic mail (E-mail) is fast mail service over computer networks. E-mail gives you the capability to send messages to anyone who has an E-mail address anywhere in the world, and they will receive your message and maybe even reply in the same day! If you have a good E-mail program with a friendly user interface, it is easy to participate in this unique medium.

An E-mail program usually has several primary functions: to send mail and reply to messages in your mailbox, to save and delete messages you receive, to insert text files into your messages, and to write one E-mail message and send it to multiple sites. Of course, the functions are not limited to these and as you learn your E-mail program you will gradually become aware of all of the options offered to you. The E-mail tool can usually be customized to meet a variety of your additional needs. If you have direct access to the Internet, you probably will want to use a program for E-mail such as Qualcomm's *Eudora or* Microsoft's *Internet Mail*. These have all of the functions mentioned above, and more, and are available over the Web from QUALCOMM, Inc. or Microsoft Corporation. The URL addresses are given below:

http:/www.eudora.com
http://www.microsoft.com

MAILING LISTS

Mailing lists and newsgroups have their origins in the academic community, where scholars and researchers have used them to exchange ideas for years. With the widening of the Internet audience, more people than ever before may now obtain access to these scholarly discussions as well as other types of discussions of interest, giving everyone a great opportunity for broadening their education and keeping up with new ideas in the academic community and beyond. There are many mailing lists (many using *LISTSERV*) and newsgroups specializing in various psychology topics, and they are available to the general public.

Electronic mailing lists operate by having electronic mail sent to a central computer,and from there, messages are posted by electronic mail to all mailboxes on the subscriber distribution list. To subscribe to a mailing list you need two addresses--the *LISTSERV* address for administrative business such as signing on, and the list address for sending messages to all of the people who have subscribed to the mailing list. Depending on the amount of activity, you may receive daily postings which sometimes create lively discussions.

There are several types of psychology mailing lists. Some psychology mailing lists have been created to allow researchers to exchange ideas and engage in collaborative work. The topics are very specialized, e.g., forensic psychiatry, geriatric neuropsychology, language theories. For many of these mailing lists, subscriptions are limited to professionals only, but by inquiring, you may be able to find out whether psychology students are allowed to subscribe.. Other mailing lists have been created to operate like "support groups." Many of these mailing lists are open to the general public. They are devoted to a particular psychological disorder (e.g., depression, schizophrenia), so that one afflicted with, or dealing with the disorder, can engage in discussions.

To subscribe to a mailing list usually requires only one E-mail message to the list moderator, who will add your name to the list if you are eligible, and send directions for participating. You can link to a number of psychology-related mailing lists from many of the master psychology sites listed in Appendix B. When choosing which mailing lists to subscribe to, keep in mind that subscribing to only a few mailing lists could result in 50-100 messages filling your mailbox daily! Remember, too, that whatever you post to a list may be distributed to thousands of subscribers.

Anyone can set up a mailing list on a local network to serve a smaller audience, such as a community organization or class in psychology at a university.

NEWSGROUPS AND DISCUSSION FORUMS
Newsgroups and a similar type of communication form, often called "discussion forums", have become a popular way to discuss a relevant topic in psychology. Asynchronous text input is used to create streams of messages which resemble a discussion. The reader of articles in a newsgroup can step in at any time to browse the messages that are currently archived and then choose whether or not to reply. An advantage of newsgroups is that your mailbox doesn't fill up with messages coming from a list; the disadvantage is that you are not notified of new articles arriving in a newsgroup, and so you must remember to check for new articles regularly. Just as with mailing lists, there are newsgroups for every need, and many of the newsgroups have been connected with their counterpart mailing list so that messages to one are automatically forwarded to the other. In addition, many newsgroups have a moderator who screens inputs before they are posted to the group.

You should be aware that many, if not most newsgroups, are not available to the average university, government, or business user. Some newsgroups are considered to be inappropriate in certain contexts due to the specific content or to the overhead required to store the newsgroup articles. Individuals are not required to subscribe to a newsgroup, but their Internet provider must carry the newsgroup on its news server. Each USENET site makes its own decisions about the set of newsgroups available to its users, so you may have to request your Internet service provider to include a newsgroup in its available selections.

Newsgroup names have several descriptive components divided by periods. The components become more specific as you read from left to right. A large number of psychology newsgroups begin with *sci.psychology.* and have a third component which describes the specific topic (e.g., consciousness, personality, etc.). One newsgroup of interest to students of psychology is *sci.psychology.research.* You can derive from this newsgroup's name that it includes the scientific psychology community and that issues are research-related. Upon reading the group's charter, you will find that discussions center around topics such as applied psychological techniques, current theoretical work, reviews of current journal articles, and grant searches. It is moderated to screen out non-psychology articles, personal attacks, political debate, and inappropriate topics such as issues related to individuals seeking help on a specific psychological disorder. To find out the purpose of the group and submission guidelines, access the *Charter of sci.psychology.research* at the following URL address:

http://www.grohol.com/spr/

The *sci.psychology.research* newsgroup also has a good set of frequently asked questions (FAQs) about psychology and psychology newsgroups. You can reach this set of questions and answers by using the search function at the *Usenet FAQs* site, located at the following URL address:

http://www.cis.ohio-state.edu/hypertext/faq/usenet/top.html

7

In addition to the *sci.psychology* newsgroups there are many newsgroups that begin with the name *alt.psychology* which are devoted to specific psychology topics, such as Jung. Self-help psychology newsgroups begin with *alt.support* and *alt.recovery*. These newsgroups serve as support groups for families with mental illness, abusers, recovering addicts, etc. By far, the best place for getting a complete listing of psychology newsgroups is the psychology site, *Psych Central*, which will link you to every known mailing list and newsgroup in the mental health and self-help areas. The lists are divided into two categories: "general support" and "professional." The professional lists are designed for individuals doing research or clinical work and carry prerequisites for joining, and the other category is for the general public. You will be able to link to each newsgroup moderator from the *Psych Central* site, but be aware that the lists change frequently because new newsgroups are often started and other groups become disbanded through lack of use. The URL address for *Psych Central* is:

http://grohol.com

Many mailing lists and newsgroups will give you information about participation after you join. If not, it is wise for a novice to start by listening and observing before posting any messages to find out the particular conventions of a group. A quick way to find out the knowledge level or restrictions of the group is to check the FAQ file or a summary of past discussion topics, if these have been archived and are available. Then, use care in composing messages so that they are clear expressions of your ideas and are courteous. In addition, take the time to decide whether it would be more appropriate to send your message to the entire group or to respond to only one person via his or her E-mail address. Responses to individuals cut down on message traffic and may often be the better choice.

Discussion forums other than newsgroups also exist on the Internet. For example, Russ Dewey, host of *Psych Web*, has implemented a number of "discussion pages." The discussion pages are open to all *Psych Web*

8

visitors, but the discussion topics are of special interest to undergraduate psychology students. Topics are of the sort likely to be found in any psychology class, such as "How Advertizers Use Classical Conditioning." If you want to make a contribution, you can click on the "feedback" button at the bottom of each page. These are moderated pages and so your contribution will be reviewed before posting by Dr. Dewey.

GETTING CONNECTED
Hopefully your school or local library will already have computers designated for Internet use. Then you can try out Internet applications and decide how you can use the Internet for your own purposes. If you decide to configure your own system, you will be aware of the minimum requirements for computer equipment and software to get the Internet capabilities you desire. Of course, there are a variety of ways to configure the system. With the bare minimum you get a connection for text-based E-mail; with add-ons and higher level Internet connectivity options, you get more enjoyable browsing and greater capabilities, such as real-time video. The company or school that is providing network access also determines the Internet services you will have and what capabilities you will use.

If you want to do more on the Internet and do it faster, then the following PC configuration will give you some extra capabilities and allow you to use more of the capabilities of the advanced Web browsers. A typical configuration will consist of a 100 MHZ *Pentium* processor, Super 32-bit VGA monitor, *Windows '95,* 16-32 MB of RAM, 1000 MB of hard disk, a sound card, microphone/speakers, and a 28,800 bps modem. With this set-up and an advanced Web browser like *Netscape Navigator 3.0,* you could hear music and voice from Web Pages with embedded audio and conduct high-quality audio conferencing.

It is very important to carefully review the capabilities of the state-of-the-art Web browser software that you plan to use to access the Web. Although there are several browsers available, the two most widely used browsers are *Microsoft Internet Explorer* and *Netscape Navigator*. The more recent versions of these browsers have much greater capabilities than earlier versions, so you can do more with them. For example, you can print from the screen with *Netscape Navigator 3.0*, but can't with version *1.0*. Even the most up-to-date browsers do not include all of the software that you will need to take advantage of all of the components of the Internet, or to access all of the information on the Internet. Usually though, the browser allows the supporting software to be identified and called from the browser itself.

The best way to get access to the Internet is to get a PPP (Point-to-Point Protocol) account with a company or school that has network access. With a stand-alone computer and modem, you will then be able to dial a phone number to get a connection to their local computer network which is connected to the global Internet network. You can run your software, called "client" programs, which will interact with "server" programs on the other computer. You need a number of software programs to make the Internet connection, so it is best to take the service provider's suggestions on which programs will work best with their "servers." Typically, they will provide many of the software packages that are known to work with their system.

You may also get access to the Internet through an Internet service provider, a company that has the computers and leased lines to act as your gateway to the Internet. For example, *America Online* provides Internet access among other online services. There are several providers who provide Internet access only. Either way, you pay a monthly fee to "dial in" to access the online services. Most service providers will give you access to the Web and E-mail services for one or more persons, but they may not offer some of the other services such as FTP, Gopher, WAIS, and USENET.

While the Web at first glance seems very complex and potentially difficult to use, the best approach is to get on the Web and become familiar with it. It is both fun and educational.

CHAPTER 2
CONDUCTING RESEARCH ON THE INTERNET

The Internet can bring you the latest research and discussion on "hot" topics in psychology. The Net gives you a window to "living" psychology where you quickly gain a sense of how practitioners and researchers around the world live and breathe psychology in their daily lives. Information on the Internet is less than a year old, in most cases, and updates are frequent.   In that sense, the Internet is not like a college library, full of the history and traditions of psychology. Instead, you get the psychology of the "here and now." A keyword search on the Internet is very likely to lead you to an article in a recently published psychology newsletter, or a list of the current research projects at a renowned research institute. Searches often lead to another important source of information on the Internet--the popular *USENET* newsgroups on a large variety of psychology-related subjects. Here you'll find discussions of current issues in psychology as viewed by academicians and practitioners, or you can become part of a support group for the general public. Mailing lists and newsgroups were discussed in detail in Chapter 1.

The Internet is not as mysterious or difficult to use as it first seems to the novice. However, with the number of Web pages growing daily, searching for information is becoming cumbersome. As a student of psychology, you need to know how to do efficient searches and how to sift through the various types of resources that are available. Information on the Internet is distributed from a variety of sources in a variety of styles. Just to name a few, there are mental health articles designed to be "brochures" for the general public, research articles, book reviews, news articles, and abstracts (short summaries of articles) designed for professionals. In order to better evaluate the information you receive, you need to know something about the purpose and sources of these various types of information.

MASTER SITES AND OTHER WEB SITES FOR GENERAL PSYCHOLOGY

In the past, the purpose of the Internet centered on the exchange of science and research information; use of the Internet for commercial purposes, such as product advertisement, was frowned upon. Today, the basic infrastructure of the "network of networks" is changing hands--moving from government and education networks to commercial and special interest networks. With the commercialization of the Internet, the number of Web sites is growing at a staggering rate, and it now takes longer to find scholarly and scientific information. To save time and make your travels on the "information highway" more efficient, Appendix B presents a number of "master" sites for general psychology. These sites are so named because they have an extensive number of links to resources about general academic topics in psychology. They have so much information that you will want to "bookmark" these sources so that you can return to them again and again. Since the master sites are likely to become some of your "favorite places" on the Web, use your browser to save their URL addresses for future use.

Publishers of psychology textbooks provide another important source of general academic information about psychology. You can go to any of these publishers' Web sites to find Web pages designed to accompany one or more of their psychology textbooks. For example, Longman's *PsychZone* offers numerous links to psychology resources, organized according to major psychology topics. You can reach *PsychZone* by using the following URL address:

http://longman.awl.com/psychzone/

To make searching for psychology information on the Web even easier, Chapter 3 provides over a hundred Web sites on specific psychology topics. The Web sites are organized according to academic areas typically found in general psychology textbooks. These resources present articles, interactive exercises, demonstrations, and references on hundreds of specialized psychology topics.

The master sites and other Web sites for general psychology were selected because they are sponsored by reputable educational institutions and professional organizations, and because the sites provide reliable educational and professional resources. These sites have teachers, students, researchers and professionals as their intended audience, and the informational resources are of an academic or professional nature.

The remainder of this chapter shows you the types of information available through these sites. If after searching these sites you still have not found the information you need, then it is suggested that you use one of the many search tools available through your Web browser. Since the Internet is largely unregulated, remember to always evaluate your findings by considering the source. Ask yourself the following questions: Who is providing the information? What are their credentials? Is the source reputable? Who is the intended audience?

When reading information on the Web, be critical. Just because there is a Web site doesn't mean the information at that site is correct. Information in printed form must pass before the critical eyes of reviewers, editors, and publishers. Many articles on the Web may not have been through a review process, so beware, and use your best judgment!

SEARCH TOOLS
It is possible to search directly for information on a particular topic in psychology by using a search tool, or "search engine", as they are sometimes called. Typical Web-based search tools let you type in a keyword, and the program will then immediately conduct a search of the Web.

If you are using an advanced Web browser, like *Netscape Navigator 3.0*, you will be able to click on an icon which will provide you with several search tools to choose from. One of the most powerful search tools is *AltaVista* which searches the full text of Web documents and *USENET* newsgroups. *AltaVista* indexes all words, including common words and definite articles, and so is able to find exact phrases such as "all-or-none-response" (a phrase used to explain neurons.)

The various search engines are designed differently. *WebCrawler* searches its index, which it updates daily. The index is based on page titles and URL contents only , which means you get fewer "hits," but they are likely to be very close to what you are looking for. *Excite* searches several million Web pages and thousands of Web site listings and *USENET* postings, and uses Intelligent Concept Extraction (ICE) which relates your key word to other words on the Web that are similar in concept. Here you are likely to get an unwieldy, large number of "hits." *Yahoo* has a very extensive hierarchical topical index which may lead you to relevant "hits" quickly. With its small number of topical categories, it can be browsed as well as searched. But, *Yahoo* is manually maintained and covers only a very small percentage of Web sites. *WebCrawler* can search for words that are near or adjacent to one another. For instance, you can type "schizophrenia NEAR/10 genetics" to locate documents in which both words appear within 10 words of each other, in either direction. With *HotBot,* you can type in a URL address and it will give you the addresses of all links to that address. Some of the search engines allow searches of multimedia files on the Internet. You can search for pictures with *HotBot* and *Lycos.*

As with any search function, very specific keywords may result in no findings. If this happens, use a more general keyword to increase your chances of finding related information. Each search tool has information on how to use the query language to get the best results. This information is usually in the Help section.

The search engines can be accessed directly through their URL addresses. Some of the addresses are listed below:

http://www.altavista.digital.com
http://Webcrawler.com.html
http://www.excite.com
http://www.yahoo.com
http://www.hotbot.com

Most search services are free to the user and rely on advertising revenues. This may all change with the ever increasing load on the free search servers. In the future, many users may gladly pay a service charge to save time when conducting searches.

DATABASES AND ARCHIVES

The American Psychological Association (APA) maintains very large databases containing abstracts of articles from psychology-related journals. Libraries or institutions usually purchase these databases and the systems to search. The cost is prohibitive for individuals. But the APA Web site is a large database in and of itself. Recently, the APA has created a new search engine, called *PsychCrawler,* that can search the APA Web site. You will get information in various forms, sometimes just a title and reference of a journal article, and other times a full article, such as a book review.

The Counseling in Primary Care Trust in Great Britain has created a free search service called *Counsel.Lit.* You can search a database of almost 2,000 entries, including journal articles, reviews, and research abstracts related to counseling in primary care. Their URL address is:

http://psyctc1.sghms.ac.uk/

Child Development Abstracts & Bibliography: Online Edition, published by the University of Chicago Press for the Society for Research in Child Development, is now available for a trial period. Here you can search current issues and available back issues. The URL address is:

http://www.journals.uchicago.edu/CDAB/journal/index.html

Guenther, at the University of Augsburg, Germany, has created a search tool called *Psycharticle Search* which can search for full articles in APA journals, the *MEDLINE* database and other databases. You can access this search tool at the following URL address:

http://www.wiso.uni-augsburg.de/sozio/hartmann/psycho/jsearch.html

For anyone interested in medical or psychiatric information, archives from the American Medical Association (AMA) journals can be searched through the *AMA-Journal Search Form* located at the following URL address:

http://www.ama-assn.org/cgi-bin/search

Internet resources related to psychology can be found by using a service of the National Library of Medicine (NLM) to search 9 million citations in the *Medline* database. You will get a short abstract of a published article and the reference information to find it in a library. The URL address of this search service is:

http://www4.ncbi.nlm.nih.gov/PubMed

Another specialized free search service has been developed by the National Mental Health Services. Their *Knowledge Exchange Network (KEN)* is designed to be a one-stop source. You can currently search the Web pages of 1,800 private organizations and government agencies that provide mental health services and information. *KEN* has recently added two new searchable databases to their Web site: the Consumer/Survivor Database and the 1995 Mental Health Directory. Their URL address is:

http://www.mentalhealth.org

A frequently searched database pertaining to education research is the Educational Research Information Clearinghouse (ERIC). You can search this database using *AskERIC* to find useful reports and then request copies of full-reports, which will be provided for a fee. To use *AskERIC,* go to the following URL address:

http://www.askeric.org/

ELECTRONIC JOURNALS

The term "electronic journal" is seen frequently as one browses the Web sites related to psychology, but there is little consistency in how the term is being used. In a conservative sense, electronic journals are viewed as electronic versions of the "paper" journals archived in our public libraries. But in many ways, this is a narrow view when one considers the multimedia opportunities the Internet provides. A more visionary view of electronic publishing includes presentation of visual and auditory information, easy archiving of past issues, searchable indices, hyperlinks to related information, and fast peer feedback, just to name a few of the possibilities.

For example, Cambridge University Press maintains an electronic journal called *Behavioral and Brain Sciences (BBS) Target Article Preprints.* The paper version of the journal publishes controversial articles in biology, cognitive science, artificial intelligence, linguistics, and philosophy. Articles are peers-reviewed, and if accepted, commentaries are invited. The commentaries, the target article, and the author's responses are then co-published. You can preview current and upcoming articles by accessing the following URL address:

http://cogsci.soton.ac.uk/~harnad/bbs.html

Psycoloquy is an electronic journal sponsored by the APA and it has a format similar to the *BBS*. The journal publishes refereed articles and peer commentary. You can reach this journal through the following URL address:

http://www.princeton.edu/~harnad/psyc.html

ECT On-Line is an electronic journal from Great Britain open to writing and discussion on the topic of electroshock therapy. The journal has written instructions for submission of articles, which are peer reviewed, and presents abstracts of all articles accepted for publication online. You can reach the site of this journal at the following URL address:

http://www.priory.co.uk/journals/psych/ectol.htm#links

Most psychology journals in paper form can be found on the Internet, but the journals vary tremendously in the amount of information that they publish online. Some provide only a table of contents of each issue, while others provide abstracts only. In these cases, an actual article must be obtained from the "paper" journal. Only a few present full articles online, and the numbers may vary from one article per issue, a few select articles, or the entire issue. If you ever need quick access to a good list of psychology journals, the psychology master sites in Appendix B provide some excellent ones. The lists of journals have been created so that if you click on a name of a journal on the list you will get subscription information, but many of the lists will also give you online access to the journals' tables of contents and/or abstracts of articles. If the journal puts self-contained articles on the Web, it will be possible to access the article immediately. *PsycSite* has links to two very comprehensive journal lists, one published by Guenther and the other by Krantz for the American Psychological Society (APS). Using Guenther's list of almost 1000 links to psychology and social science journal sites, you can use a search tool to go directly to journals in a category (e.g., clinical psychology). From there you can view all of the listed journals or narrow your list to only those containing full-text articles. Using the APS list, you can search psychology-related journals listed in alphabetical order by journal name and find out immediately whether you can access a table of contents, subscription information only, abstracts, and/or full-text articles.

18

LIBRARY CATALOGS
One way to find information on a given topic is to go to a library and use its catalog. The Internet gives you the opportunity to search several library catalogs while sitting at your computer. If the catalog search results in an article or book that you are interested in, you usually can get it through interlibrary loan. *CyberPsychLink* has a good list of library catalogs that allow online access to the general public.

The *Library of Congress Information System* offers Web-based Z39.50 client interfaces to over 90 online library catalogs and databases inside and outside the Library of Congress. You can reach this service at the following URL address:

http://lcWeb.loc.gov/homepage/online.html

Many state government libraries and state university libraries also offer Z39.50 search tools.

SOFTWARE AND SHAREWARE
A variety of software to conduct experiments, present computer simulations, and analyze classroom data, etc. can be obtained over the Web. Sometimes software (trialware) can be downloaded and used for a trial period absolutely free, giving you a chance to evaluate its usefulness. This software may sometimes be just a "demo", or may have some features that are disabled until you pay to use them (crippleware). Shareware is usually copyrighted and it is best to pay the requested fee to avoid potential problems in the future. Catalogs of software for psychology which describe software packages and give purchase information are available online through *PsycLink*. The URL address is:

http://www.plattsburgh.edu/psyclink

The *CTI Directory of Psychology Software*, based in the United Kingdom, has software indexed by psychology courses or you can search the alphabetical listing. Descriptions of the packages are provided.. The URL address is:

http://www.york.ac.uk/inst/ctipsych/web/CTI/SearchDir.html

PsycSite has a list of resources that will point you to several sites where you can browse catalogs or download programs.

Another good Web site for access to shareware is called *Shrink Tank*. This is a shareware list that contains lots of interesting questionnaires and psychological tests in the form of executable or program files for PC/MS DOS-type computers. You can download personality tests and rating scales that measure assertiveness, empathy, compulsive debtor tendencies, etc. The files are zipped (compressed) files and the program to unpack (decompress) the files is provided. You can download the programs to your own computer and then use them whenever you want to. Remember that shareware programs often have imperfections in the programming. Also, there frequently will be a request for donations. You can access this site with the following URL address:

http://www.shrinktank.com/psyfiles.htm

TIPS FOR WRITING PAPERS
PsycSite includes a "Student Centre" which provides pointers to sites of special relevance to psychology students. You will be directed to useful information about the *American Psychological Association Style Manual* and other sources of advice for writing papers. The *Psychology Jumping Stand* and *Psych Web* also have resources related to preparing papers and oral presentations.

If you will be writing a research report or term paper and will be using Internet information, you will have to know about the current standards for referencing electronically-published information. *PsychREF* has quite a few links to helpful resources, and the APA has provided examples of a variety of Web citations in acceptable APA style. You can access these examples at the following URL address:

http://www.apa.org/jounals/faq.html

The Web and other advances in digital technology have dramatically increased the ease with which "intellectual property" can be changed and reproduced, making copyright violations and plagiarism a cause for concern.   Do not use Internet information in your papers and presentations without referencing it.   Authors of materials published through the Internet are protected by federal copyright laws.

Also keep in mind that, although there is free access to most Internet information, the material cannot be reproduced in large numbers in the form of "hard copy" without the author's permission. It has been suggested that federal copyright laws should be changed to better protect the rights of publishers on the Internet.

CHAPTER 3
COURSE-RELATED WEB SITES

There is a wide variety of scholarly information on the Internet intended for the academic community and professionals in the field. The Internet links in this chapter will provide you with hundreds of scholarly resources. The resources are sorted by academic topics similar to the topical divisions of many general psychology textbooks. The value of Internet information is that it is often presented in a multimedia format and is sometimes interactive. The resources will direct you to graphic, video, and sound presentations, and in some cases, you will be able to interact with the material and receive feedback. Of course, most of academic psychology remains offline rather than on the Internet itself, and so the resources will direct you to psychology books, magazines, and journals to help you get to information in print form, as well.

If you have trouble linking to a site on this list, try again later. Many times a site may appear to be dead, but it may simply be that the server is down temporarily.

HISTORY OF PSYCHOLOGY
American Psychological Association: (Division 26) History of Psychology
http://www.yorku.ca/dept/psych/orgs/apa26/
Besides having a list of several Internet links related to the history of psychology, the site contains current articles related to this topic from the Division 26 newsletter published online.

Canadian Psychological Association: History and Philosophy of Psychology
http://www.yorku.ca/dept/psych/orgs/cpa25.htm

The association publishes their Section 25 History and Philosophy of Psychology bulletin on the Net. At this site you can access current articles related to the history of psychology.

History of Psychology
http://server.bmod.athabascau.ca/html/aupr/history.htm
The site has an extensive number of Internet links to history of psychology resources, including a link to a history of medicine searchable database.

Mind and Body: Rene Descartes to William James
http://serendip.brynmawr.edu/Mind/Table.html
This site presents lengthy discussions about mind/body dualism, the rise of experimental psychology, and the beginnings of American psychology. Excellent graphics make the text more enjoyable to read.

Resources in the History of Psychology
http://198.49.179.4/pages/awalsh/psych-history.html
This site includes a history of psychology timetable, historic milestones in neuroscience, and a short history of lobotomy.

Today in the History of Psychology
http://www.cwu.edu/~warren/today.html
This site, developed by Warren Street, enables you to view selected events in the history of psychology for any day of the year by clicking on "pick a date."

THE SCIENCE OF PSYCHOLOGY
The Amazing Randi
http://www.randi.org
This site, sponsored by Florida's James Randi Educational Foundation, promotes a philosopy of rationalism and is devoted to the debunking of paranormal psychology claims. Scholarships are offered for student essays,

and Randi's show is broadcast live on the Internet. The foundation hopes to conduct and finance basic research in paranormal psychology.

On Being a Scientist: Responsible Conduct in Research
http://www.nas.edu/readingroom/books/obas
This is an HTML version of a book on research ethics published by a joint committee of the National Academy of Sciences, the National Academy of Engineers, and the Institute of Medicine. The material is suitable for classes on research methods or the philosophy of science.

Pitfalls of Data Analysis
http://maddog.fammed.wisc.edu/pitfalls/
This resource is an article about statistics and how to use them to make clear and accurate conclusions. Examples come from medicine, education and industry. The paper was part of a workshop at the Third International Applied Statistics in Industry Conference in Dallas, Texas, June, 1995.

The Random Research Question Generator
http://www.coedu.usf.edu/behavior/research/research.html
This a humorous, tongue-in-cheeck site from the University of South Florida which randomly generates hypotheses for research. Users are invited to contribute their own independent variables and dependent variables to the "research question" generator.

The Skeptic's Dictionary
http://dcn.davis.ca.us/~btcarrol/skeptic/dictcont.html
Robert T. Carrol, Professor of Philosophy, has put together a page of links related to skepticism and rational argument against occult claims, including such topics as tarot cards, alien abductions, ESP, ghosts, etc.

WWW-Sites for Experimental Psychology
http://www.psychologie.uni-bonn.de/allgm/links.htm
This German site is a good place to get an overview of the science of psychology. There are a number of links related to experimental

psychology organized into topical categories that will lead you to online documents, journals, and institutes and societies. From this site you can also link to a few experiments on the Internet.

BIOLOGICAL BASIS OF BEHAVIOR
Behavioral and Brain Sciences (BBS) Target Article Preprints
http://www.princeton.edu/~harnad/bbs.html
BBS electronically publishes interdisciplinary "target articles" in psychology, neuroscience, behavioral biology, cognitive science, artificial intelligence, lignuistics, and philosophy. Archived articles can be searched using a key-phrase index, author index, or full-text search.

Institute for Brain Aging and Dementia
http://www.alz.uci.edu
This University of California at Irvine site specializes in the problems of dementia including Alzheimer's disease. Although there are few links to other sites, this site provides comprehensive information pages about the causes and diagnosis of dementia, brain imaging data, and useful product information.

Neuroimaging Primer
http://www.med.harvard.edu/AANLIB/hms1.html
The site presents lecture notes from the Harvard Medical School: Introduction to Neuroimaging course.

Neuropsychology Central
http://www.premier.net/~cogito/neuropsy.html
The site is a very comprehensive set of resources pertaining to the understanding, diagnosis, and treatment of neuropsychological disorders (categorized by disorder). Developmental and geriatric resources are included. Research articles from major neuropsychological laboratories in the U.S. and abroad, self-help fact sheets, and lists of support organizations can be found at this site.

Neuropsychology Study Aid
http://www.uta.fi/~tk54334/neurops.html
This excellent Finnish site provides an interesting set of neuroscience links.
The links are organized as a table of contents for a neuropsychology text
with chapters on the nervous system, brain, imaging, sensation, diseases,
and drugs.

Neuroscience
http://neuro.med.cornell.edu/VL/
Supported by the Department of Neurology and Neuroscience at Cornell
University Medical College, the site is a component of the World-Wide
Web Virtual Library. Resources are listed alphabetically by provider or
resource, as appropriate.

Neuroscience Connections
http://www.jmu.edu/psyc/neuro/index.html
This James Madison University Web site presents resources for learning
neuroscience fundamentals and the biological mechanisms and treatment of
mental disorders.

Neurosciences on the Internet
http://www.neuroguide.com
The site contains a searchable and browsable index of neurosciences
available on the Internet. The database can be accessed by browsing, by
searching by title, keyword, or URL, or by playing Neuroroulette.
Neurobiology, neurology, neurosurgery, psychiatry, psychology, cognitive
science, and human neurological diseases are covered.

SENSATION AND PERCEPTION
Auditory Perception: Demonstrations and Experiments
http://www.music.mcgill.ca/auditory/Auditory.html

This site is a multimedia presentation of selected topics in auditory perception, such as pitch perception, auditory scene analysis, and the Tritone Paradox. The presentations include auditory demonstrations, discussions, and experiments.

The Exploratorium
http://exploratorium.edu/
This site contains visual illusions online and also has a demonstration of the dissection of a cow's eye for those who want to understand the anatomy of an eye.

Gallery of Illusions
http://aspen.uml.edu/~landrigad/illusion.html
The site contains a menu from which you may choose many common perceptual illusions. You may link to discussions of perception-related topics and examples, such as "Organization as a Primary Characteristic of Perception."

Magic Eye--How to See 3-D
http://www.vision3d.com
The site is very comprehensive, containing references to information about common visual disabilities of children, a directory of opthamologists by state, demonstrations of 3-D vision, and instructions on how to see 3-D. Some optical illusions can be downloaded.

Perception Lab Home Page
http://www.st-and.ac.uk/~www_sa/academic/imaging/
This site presents research topics at the Perception Lab, School of Psychology, St. Andrews University, Scotland. The topics include facial ageing, facial attractiveness, facial prototyping and face recognition.

The Psychophysiology WWW Directory
http://rcf.usc.edu/~vanman/psyphy.html

This site is an international directory of psychophysiology-related Web sites. The directory is organized by geographic location. Listings are by researcher, organization, and company.

SIRDS Pages
http://www.ccc.nottingham,ac.uk/~etzpc/sirds.html
This site contains pictures, programs that can be downloaded, and information about single image random dot stereo (SIRDS) images. These are images that appear three-dimensional when viewed in the correct way. There are many links to SIRDS-related resources on the Web.

UCSC Perceptual Science Laboratory
http://mambo.ucsc.edu/
The Perceptual Science Laboratory at the University of California at Santa Cruz researches several areas of experimental and theoretical interest in the area of perception and cognition. Information is provided on a variety of topics including facial analysis, lipreading, model fitting, and computer graphics. There are several links to related topics.

Vision Science
http://www.visionscience.com/VisionScience.html
Search this site's archives to find information on conferences, institutes, departments, organizations, journals, software resources, mailing lists, and hundreds of images (which can be downloaded).

SLEEP, DREAMS, AND CONSCIOUSNESS
Hypnosis and Memory
http://www.guam.net/home/bmarmie/hypnosismem/hypmem.html
B. Marmie intends this site to be a starting point for investigating the relationship between hypnosis and memory. The site provides general facts about hypnosis and memory, and descriptions of general studies and forensic studies about this topic.

A Page of Dreams
http://lucien.berkeley.edu/dreams.html
Here you will find a very large number of links to selected sites related to dreams and dreaming, including dream images, dream counselling references, and links to various types of dream analysis.

PSYCHE: An Interdisciplinary Journal of Research on Consciousness
http://psyche.cs.monash.edu.au/
This is a refereed electronic journal on the topic of consciousness and its relationship to the brain. The journal is interdisciplinary and publishes material from several perspectives, including cognitive science, philosophy, psychology, and artificial intelligence. You can browse current issues of the journal.

Sleep Home Pages
http://bisleep.medsch.ucla.edu/
This is a very comprehensive site containing links to conference abstracts and other large databases on sleep. Here you will also find an international directory of sleep researchers and clinicians, and links to sleep-related resources. Find out about contemporary perspectives on sleep and sleep disorders.

Web of Addictions
http://www.well.com/user/woa/
The site provides access to information about alcohol and other drug addictions. It contains a collection of fact sheets, contacts with groups and organizations, in-depth topical information, and links to Net resources related to addictions.

MOTIVATION AND EMOTION
Berkeley Psychophysiology Laboratory
http://socrates.berkeley.edu/~lorenmc/bpl.html

This site contains references and abstracts about the laboratory's research related to emotion.

Drive Reduction Theory
http://www.lincoln.ac.nz/educ/tip/25.htm
Here you will find a short overview of Clark Hull's drive reduction theory and some examples and applications. The site also provides a reference list for further study.

Geneva Emotion Research Group
http://www.unige.ch/fapse/emotion/welcome.html#emoLinks
From the University of Geneva, this site lists group memers and their research interests and publications. Abstracts and some full-text articles are available. In addition, there are several links to other emotion-related research from major universitities around the world.

The Emotion Home Page
http://emotion.ces.brandeis.edu/emotion.html
This a good site to obtain academic discussions of emotion-related research from the experimental and clinical psychology perspectives. Conferences, journals, and other online resources related to emotion research are listed.

What's Your Emotional Intelligence Quotient
http://www.utne.com/cgi-bin/eq
Daniel Goldman, Harvard psychologist and author of the book, *Emotional Intelligence*, has provided a short test of emotional intelligence. After you answer the 10 questions on the test, your answers and the correct answers are discussed.

LEARNING AND MEMORY
Amnesia Research Lab
http://hermes.cns.uiuc.edu/ARLHomePage.html

This is the home page for the Amnesia Research Lab at the University of Illinois at Urbana-Champaign. The laboratory specializes in research on the organization of human memory and the neural systems underlying memory using a cognitive neuroscience approach. Current research interests include memory disorders, eye movement monitoring, and functional neuroimaging.

Behavior Analysis
http://www.coedu.usf.edu/behavior/behavior.html
The Behavior Analysis home page comes from the University of South Florida. Along with information about their graduate programs, the site gives you links to many behavior analysis resources.

Common Cents: A Memory Experiment
http://www.exploratorium.edu/memory/index.html
How many visual details of a penny can you recognize? You can take part in a demonstration of memory concepts at this site.

Computer Archives for the Study of Animal Behavior
http://www.cisab.indiana.edu
The site is provided by the Center for the Integrative Study of Animal Behavior at Indiana University. Resources are related to biology, psychology, and neuroscience.

Don't Shoot the Dog
http://karenpryor.com
This is a commercial site where the author is presenting effective teaching and training techniques that use positive reinforcement. A major part of her method is called "Clicker training," and seminars, catalogs of products, and news related to the method are available.

False Memory Syndrome Foundation
http://advicom.net/~fitz/fmsf

This site defines false memory syndrome and describes the purposes, activities, and programs of the foundation. You can also link to articles and mailing lists on the subject.

Journal of Experimental Psychology: Animal Behavior Processes
http://www.apa.org/journals/xan.html
The home page of this journal links to the table of contents and abstracts of their current issue, and past tables of content. You can also search all APA journals from this site.

Journal of the Experimental Analysis of Behavior (JEAB) and the Journal of Applied Behavioral Analysis (JABA)
http://www.envmed.rochester.edu/wwwrap/behavior/jeabjaba.htm
The journals share this Web site. JEAB publishes experiments relevant to the behavior of individual organisms and JABA publishes applications of the experimental analysis of behavior to "problems of social importance." You can search the journals' abstracts and read some full-text articles, but to do this you must first download a reader program. Video clips and audio presentations make this a multimedia site!

Learning and Memory
http://207.22.83.2:443/cshl/journals/lnm/
The journal publishes articles about the neurobiology of learning and memory and is interdisciplinary. From their home page you can access the tables of contents for recent issues, and abstracts are available for all articles starting with Volume 2, Issue 5.

Memory Techniques and Mnemonics
http://www.gasou.edu/psychweb/mtsite/memory.html
From this Web page you are able to link to a number of techniques that may significantly improve your memory. Methods to improve remembering quotations, names, and mnemonics for exams are among many of the applications of these methods.

33

Positive Reinforcement: A Self-Instructional Exercise
http://server.bmod.athabascau.ca/html/prtut/reinpair.htm
This is an interactive exercise designed to teach the prinicples of positive reinforcement. It is provided as an example of instruction from an online Psychology of Learning course from Athabascau University in Canada.

Smart Drug/Nootropic Info
http://www.damicon.fi/sd/
The site describes nootropic drugs as "a new class of drugs that act as cognitive enhancers with no side effects or toxicity." The site provides general information about "smart drugs" and links to information concerning individual nootropics, such as Gingko Biloba and Melatonin. Some user experiences are described, and there are price lists and advertisements for various products.

THINKING, LANGUAGE, AND INTELLIGENCE
American Creativity Association
http://www.becreative.org
Much of this site is still under construction. At this time you can find quotations about creativity, imagination, intuition, and other related concepts. There is a calendar with dates and information about upcoming seminars on creativity, and links to creativity-related Web sites.

The Arc, a National Organization on Mental Retardation
http://www.metronet.com/~thearc/welcome.html
The Arc home page serves about 1,100 affiliate chapters of the National Organization on Mental Retardation. Use the site's search engine to find fact sheets, advocacy materials, and services related to mental retardation and other developmental disabilities. The site also has a "discussion board" to discuss issues and share information, and there are several links to related Web sites.

The Braintainment Center
http://www.brain.com/welcome.htm
This commercial site brings you many games, tests, and discussions related to cognition, intelligence, and problem solving. It lets you try out its 5-minute intelligence test and will give you an IQ score based on your performance. The site has many products to sell that are related to these topics.

Calvin and Hobbes Game
http://www.psych.nwu.edu/~squish/ch-game.html
Northwestern University psychology enthusiasts have put together a game designed to test your problem solving abilities. Get 5 Calvins and 5 Hobbes across the river.

Cognitive Science
http://www.cudenver.edu/~mryder/itc_data/cogsci.html
This University of Colorado site provide a large number of cognitive science links that are organized around celebrities in cognitive sciences. The links include papers, archives, reviews, bibliographies, interviews, profiles, and celebrity home pages.

The Emergence of Intelligence
http://weber.u.washington.edu/~wcalvin/sciamer.html
This page will link you to an online reprint of William H. Calvin's article by the same name published in *Scientific American* in 1994. From the reprint site you can do a *Medline* search to find about 100 additional articles related to this topic.

The Gorilla Foundation
http://www.gorilla.org
The Gorilla Foundation was founded in 1976 to promote protection and propagation of gorrillas. A primary focus of the organization is Project Koko, which involes teaching a modified form of American Sign Language

35

to two gorillas. You can view numerous images of gorillas and find out more about the foundation and its work at this site.

Intelligence Tests Online
http://www.iglobal.net/psman/prstests.html#intelligence
The site lists several IQ tests that are online or that are downloadable. Some test sites may demand a fee. This not a psychology site and no attempt has been made by the Web master to determine the validity of the tests.

Skeptic Magazine Interview with Robert Sternberg on *The Bell Curve*
http://www.skeptic.com/03.3.fm-sternberg-interview.html
The resource is an article published by *Skeptic* magazine in 1995 about Sternberg's reaction to Herrnstein and Murray's controversial book about the relationship between heritability of intelligence and environmental influences on intelligence.

Two Views of the Bell Curve
http://www.apa.org/journals/bell.html
The site contains two reviews, by Thomas J. Bouchard, Jr. and Donald D. Dorfman, of the controersial best seller, *The Bell Curve,* by Richard J. Herrnstein and Charles Murray. Of course, one review is favorable and one is not.

DEVELOPMENTAL PSYCHOLOGY
Adolescence: Change and Continuity
http://www.personal.psu.edu/faculty/n/x/nxd10/adolesce.htm
This site was developed by students taking the Transition to Adulthood course at Pennsylvania State University. The students provide detailed information about the social, biological, and psychological influences on adolescents at puberty.

Adolescence Directory On-Line
http://education.indiana,edu/cas/adol/adol.html
This site at the Center for Adolescent Studies at Indiana University
provides an electronic guide to information about adolescent issues. The
site is intended for educators, counselors, parents, researchers, health
practitioners, and teens. The links are organized around the themes of
conflict and violence, mental health, health, counseling, and teens only.

AgeNet Homepage
http://home.earthlink.net/~abbottam/gerontology.htm
AgeNet promotes itself as the complete source for aging and
gerontological resources. The links and information are organized in the
areas of theories of aging, long-term care, public policy, and internet
resources. Links are provided sites with information about professional
associations, long-term care, Alzheimers, research, ocial security, and
Medicare.

American Academy of Child and Adolescent Psychiatry (AACAP)
http://www.aacap.org/web/acap/
This is the site of a reputable national organization for professionals with a
psychiatric approach to the diagnosis and treatment of childhood disorders.
The AACAP publishes online *Facts for Families (FFF)* brochures to
educate parents and families about psychiatric disorders affecting children
and adolescents.

APA Division 20 Adult Development and Aging
http://www.iog.wayne.edu/APADIV20/APADIV20.htm
This site is hosted by the Institute of Gerontology at Wayne State
University. This site contains information about Division 20, employment
opportunities, programs of study, instructional resources for teachers of
aging, resources for clinicians, and links to other Web sites devoted to
aging.

Center for Adolescent Studies
http://education.indiana.edu/cas/cashmpg.html
This site contains a variety of links for educators, counselors, researchers, health professionals, parents and teachers. These resources include information about physical and mental health, social issues, counseling, education, risky behavior, drug abuse, and normal behavior.

Classic Theories in Child Development
http://www.idealist.com/children/cdw.html
This site contains overviews of the theories of Margaret Mahler, Sigmund Freud & Erik Erikson. There is also a month-by-month look at development during early childhood, and links to other child development-related resources.

Directory of WEB and Gopher Sites on Aging
http://www.aoa.dhhs.gov/aoa/webres/craig.htm
This a master site for aging maintained by the U.S. Department of Health and Human Services. There are currently over 2000 external links. The site is not organized by aging topic, but instead provides links to academic and research institutions, non-profit organizations, consultants, and businesses involved with aging issues.

Internet and E-mail Resources on Aging
http://www.aoa.dhhs.gov/jpost6/generalresources.html
This is another master site maintained by the U.S. Department of Health and Human Services. The resources are organized by aging topic. Topics covered include aging in general, Alzheimer's and related disorders, death and dying, family organizations, geriatrics, health, leisure, and retirement. The links include master sites, newsgroups, organizations, publications, and conferences both in the U.S. and other countries.

Gerontological Society of America
http://www.geron.org

The Gerontological Society sponsors this site to promote the scientific study of aging. Topics include conferences, news releases, legislative updates, general information, and information for students and professionals in the field of gerontology.

GeroWeb
http://www.iog.wayne.edu/GeroWebd/GeroWeb.html
This site is maintained by the Institute of Gerontology at Wayne State University. The stated purpose of GeroWeb is to provide an online resource for researchers, educators, practitioners, and others interested in aging and older individuals. Access to the library resources at the site is through either a browser organized by topic, or a keywork search engine.

Television and Violence
http://www.ksu.edu/humec.tele.htm
Several discussions and articles pertaining to the research on children and television violence are presented here. The Web page is provided by Kansas State University.

HUMAN SEXUALITY AND GENDER DIFFERENCES
Center for Sex Research
http://www.csun.edu/~sr2022/index.html
This is the home page for the Center for Sex Research at California State University at Northridge. This site contains information about events, conferences, and other sexuality resources online.

Feminism and Women's Studies
http://english-www.hss.cmu.edu/feminism
This site contains links to women's studies and feminist works, focusing on issues of sex, gender, sexual identity, and sexuality in a cultural context.

Feminist Yellow Pages of Cyberspace
http://www.echonyc.com/~women/yellowpages.html

This feminist site contains links to a variety of other site dealing with women's issues. The sight has several search engines. The links are arranged topically, and include databases, women and performance art, feminist activist pages online, women and activism, gay resources, health, disability resources and commercial services.

Gender-related Electronic Forums
http://www-unix.umbc.edu/~korenman/wmst/forums.html
This site contains an annotated listing of publicly-accessible electronic forums related to women's and gender issues. The listings are organized topically, and include activism, arts and humanities, education, health, religion, science, sexuality, social science, women of color, and women's studies forums.

Men Web
http://www.vix.com/menmag
As the name implies, this site is dedicated to men's issues, and is sponsored by Men's Voices Magazine. The site is topically organized, and contains information and links concerning relationships, father's rights, men's groups, aging, health, books, questions and answers, articles, and related issues.

SexQuest
http://www.sexquest.com
This site is billed as "Your first source for sexuality information on the Web". The site contains many links including sexual advocacy, sexual health, sexuality and gender, birth control and abortion, activism, gay issues, censorship, sexual assault and rape, and education.

Sexology NetLine
http://www.netaccess.on.ca/~sexorg
This site is dedicated to the advancement of knowledge about human sexuality. The site doe not contain or have links to explicit sexual material.

The information at the site recommended only for teens and older individuals. Information and links are topically arranged, and include facts of life, sexuality questions and answers, online sexual advice, sexual references and resources, workshops and conferences, history of sexology, and sexology links.

Society for Human Sexuality
http://weber.u.washington.edu/~sfpse
This University of Washington site contains sexually explicit links, and is recommended only for those 18 and older. This site contains the largest online collection of information on human sexuality. The site contains a variety of links to other sites arranged topically, and includes information and links concerning safe sex, massage, and general sexuality issues.

Women's and Feminist Information Resources
http://asa.ugl.lib.umich.edu/chdocs/womenpolicy/feminist.html
This site lists a number of useful links to women's resources. The resources include resource guides, organizations, institutions, publications, electronic discussion groups, activist information, and legal and public policy information.

Women's Resources
http://sunsite.unc.edu/cheryb/women/wresources.html
This is a master site for links to sites dealing with women's issues, and is maintained by the University of North Carolina. The links are topically organized, and include, biographies, conferences, discussion forums, health, legal issues, organizations, parenting, pregnancy, publications, sexuality, and women's education.

Women's Studies Resources
http://www.inform.umd.edu/EdRes/Topic/WomensStudies
This site has a very comprehensive database of information and links relating to women's studies. The database contains conference information, employment opportunities, pictures, government documents,

41

film reviews, gender issues, readings, references, and links to Gopher and Web sites with information about women.

HEALTH PSYCHOLOGY
APA Division 38 Health Psychology
http://freud.apa.org/divisions/div38
This is the home page for American Psychological Association Division 38. The site maintains an set of links relating to general health, medicine, psychology, nursing, and public health.

Health Psychology and Behavioral Medicine
http://www.library,miami.edu/staff/lmc/psymed.html
This University of Miami site contains a comprehensive list of links for health psychology to include medical master sites, association, journals, stress, cardiovascular disease, and other health-related links.

Health Psychology Home Page
http://www.vanderbuilt.edu/AnS/psychology/health_psychology/healthpsych.htm
This site is located at Vanderbilt University. The stated purpose of the site is to bring a scientific perspective to the academic areas of health behavior, nutrition, psychotherapy, and alternative medicine. In general, this site provides factual information that was developed by students taking the Health Psychology and Psychology of Eating Disorders courses.

Society of Behavioral Medicine
http://socbehmed.org/sbm/sbm.htm
This purpose of this site is to provide access to online resources in behavioral medicine. The online resources include general health, discipline-specific, area-specific, and research links.

Stress Management
http://www.ivf.com/stress.html

This is a FAQ article produced by the Atlanta Reproductive Health Centre. Topics include how to become aware of stressors, and how to recognize what you can change to reduce stress.

PERSONALITY THEORIES AND PERSONALITY TESTING
Alfred Adler Institute of San Francisco
http://ourworld.compuserv.com/homepages/hstein
This Web site contains information about classical Adlerian psychology. There are a number of readings about the theory and practice of Adlerian psychology, several biographical sketches of Adler and his followers, and remembrances of other early contributors to psychology.

Buros Institute of Mental Measurement
http://www.unl.edu/buros
One of the most reputable sources of information about psychological tests is the Buros Institute of Mental Measurement at the University of Nebraska, Lincoln. Their Web site offers professional assistance to users of commercially published tests and promotes appropriate test selection and test use.

FreudNet: The A. A. Brill Library
http://plaza interport.net/nypsan
The site contains articles related to the life and work of Sigmund Freud, news and discussions of contemporary ideas in psychoanalysis, and links to the New York Psychoanalytic Institute and Society.

Goldberg Depression Inventory
http://www.cmhc.com/guide/dep2quiz.htm
Use this questionnaire to help determine if you need to see a mental health professional for diagnosis and treatment of depression.

Personal Construct Psychology
http://ksi.cpsc.ucalgary.ca?PCP/PCP.html

Information about George Kelly, one of the early personality theorists who promoted a constructivist system of psychology, can be found at this site.

Personality and Consciousness
http://www.wynja.com/giganto/psych/theoristsnf.html
Jung, Maslow, and Skinner are among the personality theorists discussed at this site. Links are given to resources related to each theorist.

The Personality Project
http://pmc.psych.nwu.edu/personality.html
This site's purpose is to "guide those interested in personality theory and research to the current personality research literature." On-line readings, information about scholarly societies and graduate training programs, and personality course syllabi are available here.

Shrink Tank
http://www.shrinktank.com/psyfiles.htm
This is a shareware list that contains lots of ineresting questionnaires and psychological tests in the form of executable or program files for PC/MS DOS-type computers. You can download personality tests and rating scales that measure assertiveness, empathy, compulsive debtor tendencies, etc. The files are zipped (compressed) and the program to unpack (decompress) the files is provided.

Testing and Assessment
http://www.apa.org/science/testing.html
The American Psychological Association has published information on guidelines and standards governing testing and assessment at this site. The FAQ page answers common questions about psychological tests, and there are links to other testing Web sites.

PSYCHOLOGICAL DISORDERS
Agoraphobia and other Mental Disorders

http://www.concentric.net/~danarius/mental.htm
The site contains articles about phobias and other types of anxiety disorders. There are many links to related journals, magazines, and self-help information. There is a very complete list of links to mental health chat groups, mailing lists, and discussion forums.

The Anxiety-Panic Internet
http://www.algy.com/anxiety/index.html
Resource are related to anxiety disorders such as panic attacks, phobias, shyness, generalized anxiety, obsessive-compulsive disorder, and post-traumatic stress. The site supports a self-help network dedicated to the "overcoming and cure of overwhelming anxiety".

Bipolar Disorder Information
http://www.pendelum.org/info.htm
The site contains an extensive number of resources related to the diagnosis and treatment of manic-depressive illness, including a very good FAQ resource. Full-text articles about bipolar disorder and writings of bipolars can be accessed from this site.

Clinical Psychology Resources
http://www.psychologie.uni-bonn.de/kap/li_home.htm
This is an outstanding German master site for clinical and abnormal psychology. The site contains information pertaining to a large number of disorders organized by type of disorder, and has a wide variety of resources about clinical assessment and psychotherapy. There is also a large amount of information related to psychophysiological disorders in a section called "Behavioral Medicine."

Divided Hearts MPD/DID Info and Support Web
http://www.dhearts.org/
Divided Hearts, a non-profit organization of those who were abused as children, has created this Web site to disseminate information about multiple personality disorder, other dissociative disorders, and much more.

This is definitely a self-help site, with links to major mental health organizations, support groups, suicide help, and discussion forums.

Dr. Ivan's Depression Central
http://www.psycom.net/depression.central.html
The site describes itself as the "Internet's clearinghouse for information on all types of depressive disorders." Resources related to major depression, bipolar disorder, cyclothymia, disthymia, and other mood disorders can be found here.

DSM-IV: Questions and Answers
http://www.psych.org/clin_res/q_a.html
Discussions of psychological disorders often refer to the official diagnostic criteria used by psychiatrists, psychologists, and other mental health professionals in the *Diagnostics Statistical Manual, 4th Edition (DSM-IV)*, published by the American Psychiatric Association. You will find answers to common questions about the DSM-IV at this site.

Mental Health.Com
http://www.mentalhealth.com/main.html
Mental Health.Com is a master site for mental health information. There are lots of self-help fact sheets and FAQs, and many links to research databases. Resources pertaining to diagnosis and treatment of mental illness are listed categorically by disorder.

Mental Health Net
http://www.cmhc.com
Mental Health Net is a master site for mental health information. The site claims to feature over 6,000 links, and provides professional and self-help information on a wide variety of disorders. Information about diagnosis and treatment options is arranged in cateories according to disorder. You can participate in discussion forums on various disorders and on issues such as "medication" at this site.

Online Psych
http://www.onlinepsych.com
Online Psych describes itself as a comprehensive information service.
Resources related to psychological disorders and treatment options are
organized into over 25 topical areas arranged alphabetically.

PSYCHOLOGICAL TREATMENT OF DISORDERS
Albert Ellis Institute
http://www.iret.org/
The site contains information about Ellis' rational-emotive therapy and a
link to a referral list of rational-emotive behavior therapists who are a
Fellow or Associate Fellow of the Institute in good standing and are state-
licensed.

American Association for Marriage and Family Therapy (AAMFT)
http://www.aamft.org
The site contains a consumer guide for information about marriage and
family therapy, and recent articles from *Family Therapy News*, a bimonthly
newspaper of the AAMFT.

Cyber-Psych
http://www.webweaver.net/psych
Cyber-Psych describes itself as a service bringing professional
psychological care and information to the online community in a non-
threatening, interactive format. A therapist directory lists practicing
psychotherapists by geographical area, and there are numerous links
allowing communication with therapists online.

Group Psychotherapy for the Layman
http://freud.tau.ac.il/~haimw/group1.html#group1
Written by a clinical psychologist and member of the Israeli Psychological
Association, this site answers FAQs about the different kinds of group

psychotherapy, how to choose a group therapist, and what is expected of group participants.

Internet Mental Health: Medication
http://www.mentalhealth.com/fr30.html
This Canadian site has information about the most common psychiatric drugs, including pharmacology, indications, contraindications, warnings, precautions, adverse effects, overdose, dosage, and Canadian research findings.

Psych Central
http://www.coil.com/~grohol
The site, also known as Dr. John Grohol's Mental Health Page, provides a comprehensive list of Internet links to psychotherapy-related and resources. The site contains a very complete list of pointers to psychology-related mailing lists and newsgroups.

Shocked: 40,000 Volts of Fun
http://www.il.net/~juli/shocked.html
At this site you will find statements from the National Institute of Health and the American Psychiatric Association about their current positions on the use of electroshock therapy (ECT) as a treatment for mental illness. There are abundant statements from ECT "survivors" and others, which expose the "truth" about ECT. There are also links to discussions of medication therapy and involuntary outpatient commitment.

Welcome to the Theories and Approaches in Psychotherapy Page
http://www.gallaudet.edu/~11mgourn
At this site, you can obtain information about a number of modern psychotherapies, including Adlerian, Gestalt, and Client-centered therapy. After the description of each therapy, related links are presented.

SOCIAL PSYCHOLOGY
Compendium of Social Psychology Web Resources
http://www.msu.edu/user/amcconne/social.html
This site provides links to several professional societies and associations related to the field of social psychology. There are also links to related journals and available software.

The Prisoner's Dilemna
http://serendip.brynmawr.edu/~ann/pd.html
You can play Prisoner's Dilemna, a classic game of cooperation vs. competition which has been studied by social psychologists and others in a variety of disciplines. Find out what is the basis of your decision-making.

Social Cognition Paper Archive and Information Center
http://www.psych.purdue.edu/~esmith/search.html
The site, maintained by Eliot R. Smith, Purdue University, contains titles, abstracts, and links to active researchers in the field of social cognition. There are also links to resources on the Web related to social psychology.

Social Influence: The Science of Persuasion and Compliance
http://www.public.asu.edu/~kelton
The Web site contains discussions and resources related to the psychological study of persuasion, compliance, and propaganda.

Social Psychology in Action
http://www.wesleyan.edu:80/psyc/psyc260/social.htm
This is a megasite for social psychology. There are great numbers of links to resources covering the major topics in this specialized field. Some of the topical categories are: prejudice, discrimination, and diversity; social influence, and romance and attraction.

Social Psychology Network
http://www.wesleyan.edu/psyc/psyc260/

Visit this Web page to find a comprehensive source of social psychology information. Find resources related to specific social psychology topics, research groups, online studies, journals, and Ph.D. programs.

Survey Research Center
http://www.princeton.edu/~abelson/indel.html
This site provides information about the survey method applied to social issues, consumer research, and policy analysis. Links are provided to master sites to reduce the total number of links, and include poll and survey data, research resources, research methods, research centers, market research, and associations.

The VALS Survey
http://future.sri.com/VALS/ovalshome.htm
Take the Values and Lifestyles Survey (VALS) at this site to classify yourself according to eight lifestyle groups and explore your consumer preferences. This a commercial site from SRI Consulting.

INDUSTRIAL-ORGANIZATIONAL PSYCHOLOGY
The Industrial-Organizational Psychologist
http://cmit.unomaha.edu/TIP/siop.html
This is the home page of The Industrial-Organizational Psychologist (TIP), the official newsletter of the Society for Industrial-Organizational Psychology. You can access the current issue of the newsletter as well as back issues, and the site is the gateway to other Internet resources related to the field.

Industrial Psychology Resource Page
http://www.ccnet.com/~bluenote/welcome.html
This is a commercial site with several links to Web resources related to industrial psychology. You can also find out about surveys and questionnaires located at the site.

Job Analysis and Personality Research
http://harvey.psyc.vt.edu
This site is located at Virginia Technological University. The site contains information and links relating to job analysis, job classification, and personality assessment in a job context.

ONET
http://www.doleta.gov/programs/onet
This U.S. Department of Labor site bills ONET as the nation's primary source for occupational information. The site contains a comprehensive database for job characteristics and worker attributes.

Organizational Development Network
http://www.odnet.org
This is the homepage of a Web-based service to support organizational development (OD) practicioners who want information about conferences, meetings, educational offerings, and training of interest. The service supports networking opportunities.

WWWIOPSY
http://gopher.ucon.edu/~wwwiopsy
This site is the home page of the Industrial-Organizational Psychology program at the University of Connecticut. The site provides useful links to sites specializing in human factors, human resources, professional societies, statistics, and publishers.

SPORT PSYCHOLOGY
APA Division 47 Exercise and Sport Psychology
http://www.psyc.unt.edu/apadiv47
This site is maintained by APA Division 47, and provides a comprehensive set of links relating to sport psychology in general, Division 47 issues, graduate training, conferences, organizations, and Web search engines.

Association for the Advancement of Applied Sports Psychology (AAASP)
http://spot.Colorado.EDU/~aaasp
The organization's purpose is to develop research, theory, and intervention strategies in sport psychology. The site promotes ethical and professional issues.

Enhanced Performance Systems (EPS) Articles
http://www.enhanced-performance.com/nideffer/articles.html
This commercial site contains a collection of articles about winning, business competition, performance, and sports psychology.

The Mental Edge
http://ultranet.com/~dupcak/mntledge.html
Designed and developed by a sport psychology consultant, this commercial site contains a description of the field of sport psychology and links to related resocurces on the Web.

Mind Tools-Sport Psychology
http://www.gasou.edu/psychweb/mtsite/page11.html
From this site you can access exercises on setting goals, imagery, concentration, and stress management, plus other tools related to sport psychology that help you "think your way to an excellent life."

Sport and Exercise Psychology
http://spot.colorado.edu/~collinsj/
This site, located at the University of Colorado at Boulder, provides sport psychology links relating to professional organizations, conferences, graduate training, mailing lists, and journals.

HUMAN FACTORS
Bad Designs
www.baddesigns.com

The site contains illustrated examples of things that are hard to use because they don't follow human factors principles. The examples use animation, graphics, and photographs.

ErgoWeb
http://www.ergoweb.com
From this commercial site you can link to ergonomic standards and guidelines, view an extensive database of ergonomics-related products and services, and read case studies of how professionals deal with specific ergonomic concerns. The site is very comprehensive and contains additional links to news, reviews, and current events, contacts and discussions, and a search tool to find what you need in ErgoWeb and across the Internet.

Human-Computer Interaction Resources on the Net
http://www.ida.liu.se/~miker/hci
This site provides a comprehensive set of links for HCI researchers and practitioners. Links include theses, jobs, events, databases, bibliographies, publications, newsgroups, labs, projects, companies, associations, guidelines, standards, education, software, and others.

Human Factors and Ergonomics Society
http://hfes.org
The Human Factors and Ergonomics Society is the premier association for professional psychologists and engineers involved in the Human Factors and Ergonomics fields. The site provides information regarding the society and the human factors field, as well as links to human factors-related academic, industrial, and government organizations, and professional societies.

Special Interest Group on Computer-Human Interaction
http://www.acm.org/sigchi
This site is the home page of a Special Interest Group on Computer-Human Interaction (SIGCHI) of the Association of Computing Machinery

(ACM). ACM/SIGCHI members are interested in the design, evaluation, implementation, and study of interactive computing systems for human use. In addition to information specific to the group, this site provides an interesting set of links to sites of interest to the human factors and human-computer interaction communities.

Usernomics
http://www.usernomics.com
This commercial site specializes in ergonomics for hardware, software, and training. Links are provided to sites that specialize in human-computer interface, human factors and ergonomics, safety, health, and environment, and instructional design and training.

CHAPTER 4
STUDENT RESOURCES ON THE WEB

Student access to the Internet provides invaluable aids to learning. Some online psychology courses are available, and there are very good online tutorials and demonstrations of psychology principles. Psychology articles on the Internet are innumerable. In addition, the Internet contains hundreds of student-centered resources which provide information about psychology as a profession, academic and career advisement, and other helpful resources for mental health and self-help.

PROFESSIONAL ORGANIZATIONS AND CONFERENCE INFORMATION
Professional psychology organizations have always been a major resource for information about professional issues and continuing education in the field of psychology. For the student of psychology, these organizations typically provide information about graduate programs, student chapters, and student research, and the organizations' newsletters and magazines typically provide job listings and updates on current events and hot issues. Now you can get all of the above on the Internet by simply accessing the home pages of these organizations and going from there. The APA and the APS home pages are listed in Appendix B. Some of the other master sites (e.g., *PsycSite* and *CyberPsychLink*) have links to other psychology organizations and societies.

From the home page of any major psychology organization, you can fill out a membership application form online and then mail it, E-mail it, or fax it; but even without membership status, you can browse the pages of the organization and gain access to abundant information. The home pages typically have links to resources designed especially for the student of psychology. For instance, the APA has a link called, "Student Info," and the APA has one called, "Graduate Student Resources." These links are for high school students, undergraduates, and those in graduate programs, and they have information about student societies, graduate programs, and tips on writing and publishing.

A good way to keep up with news in the field of psychology and current events affecting the field is to browse the online publications from the Web sites of the major professional organizations. Online articles from the *APS Bulletin* and the *APA Monitor* are often directed toward student needs and interests.

The *National Institute of Mental Health (NIMH)* home page has a "calendar of events" to provide a good list of conferences and other events related to psychology. In addition, the NIMH site will give you information on research fellowships, job openings, and grants funded by NIMH, the National Institute of Health (NIH), and other related organizations. The NIMH home page is located at the following URL address:

http://www.nimh.nih.gov

Of course, the APS and the APA are two very good sites for links to resources listing job openings, and most of the master sites provide links to employment information sources.

SELF-HELP AND MENTAL HEALTH REFERENCES
Several master sites in Appendix B provide a large number of self-help and mental health resources. For instance, *Psych Web* divides its resources into "scholarly" and "self-help" categories. *CyberPsychLink, APA,* and *Hanover College* also have large collections of links to self-help resources. Many of the links are to mental health "fact sheets" or FAQs. Users are also pointed to mailing lists and newsgroups related to self-help and mental health topics.

Fact sheets are brochure-like information presentations on various mental health topics such as schizophrenia, depression, anxiety disorders, etc.

Most are published by reputable national organizations, such as the American Academy of Child and Adolescent Psychiatry (AACAP) or the APA. For instance, the AACAP publishes online *Facts for Families (FFF)* brochures to educate parents and families about psychiatric disorders affecting children and adolescents. *Psych Web* has links to pamphlets and brochures that specialize in the psychological problems of college students. The articles are published online by student counseling centers at major universities around the country. The centers often have information about problems likely to be of concern to college students, such as sexuality, relationships, alcohol and depression. FAQ pages present in-depth information on a particular mental health topic in a question-and-answer format. Designed for the general public, the FAQs are presented in layman's terms.

Several of the master sites offer opportunities for ongoing scholarly discussion of self-help topics in *alt.support* newsgroups and "discussion forums" that can be entered into at any time. The newsgroups are often sponsored by a national organization providing advocacy and services around a particular mental disorder, such as Alzheimers disease, or mental retardation.

With the capabilities of the Internet to reach thousands of users, this medium is a valuable tool for spreading information about mental illness, a subject that is poorly understood. Many of the master sites listed in Appendix B make information about mental health and mental illness available to you in formats that are easy to understand. These sites are accessed by thousands of individuals each day who find hope in their quest to understand the problems in their lives and find support and services to help alleviate their distress.

CAREER AND ACADEMIC ADVISEMENT
Questions about psychology as a major and about psychology careers can be answered directly through Internet resources. The *APS* offers a "student affiliate" status so that students can find out more about small

grants, student research competition, student travel funding, and the mentor program. You can access the *APS* "Student Caucus" from the *APS* Web site.

Psych Web has several "tip sheets" for psychology majors, and *PsycSite* offers the "Student Centre" for information on graduate schools and other useful connections. *Psychology Jumping Stand* contains resources related to graduate schools, psychology-related careers, preparation for job interviews, and job searches. *PsychREF* has resources related to career planning and jobs, graduate school, field experiences, and internships.

ONLINE TUTORIALS AND COURSES

Many Web users are using the Web for educational purposes, and so it is not surprising to find that psychology students have an increasing number of online psychology courses to choose from. In addition, Internet and Intranet (network within an institution) technologies are useful methods for supplementing traditional classroom instruction. Several psychology tutorials covering diverse topics are available online. In the topical listings of resources in Chapter 3 you will find tutorials related to neuroscience, perception, positive reinforcement, child development, psychotherapy, and many other topics. Sometimes the tutorials are interactive exercises in which students have "hands-on" experiences and receive immediate feedback as they interact.

There are several complete psychology courses online. Some of the characteristic features of the Internet courses include class assignments which involve online searches, interacting with students in online discussion forums, conducting a laboratory exercise or tutorial from a remote site, and immediate feedback from online quizzes. Indiana University has a good description of their online course in General Psychology available at the *Psychology Jumping Stand. PsychREF* has a listing of several courses and tutorials online. For most of the courses, the professor has created a home page with links to the syllabus, details regarding assignments, and sometimes lecture notes. Most have an E-mail link to the professor as well. Some of the courses offer academic credit to students not enrolled at the originating school. You can visit the home page of any one of these courses to find out more about the course.

APPENDIX A
GLOSSARY OF TERMS

bookmark A function of the Internet browser that lets you set a placeholder for a particular Web address so that you can return to it easily.

browser Software that lets you view Web pages.

client According to the client-server model, software that requests services from another computer (server).

download Using a browser or FTP program, getting software to your computer from another.

FAQ Frequently Asked Questions is a document that covers basic information about a topic or discussion group in a question-and-answer format.

FTP File Transfer Protocol is software for moving files from one computer to another. Some FTP servers allow public log-on by *Anonymous FTP* procedures.

Gopher A program that provides access to organized Internet resources by having the user move through hierarchical menus.

HTML Hypertext Markup Language used to write documents that appear on the *Web* specifying format, graphics, and links to other documents.

HTTP HyperText Transfer Protocol for information transmission between computers that use the *World Wide Web*.

LISTSERV   A program that manages electronic mailing lists and their distribution functions.

newsgroup   The name used to describe a topical discussion group that is part of a world-wide network, USENET.

server   According to the client-server model, software that answers requests from a client program.

URL Uniform Resources Locator standard format for indicating addresses of Internet sites by describing information transmission protocol, the exact location of the file, and the file name.

USENET   A world-wide network of newsgroups using NNTP protocol for the exchange of messages over the Internet.   An Internet service provider must have a USENET server to provide this service to its client customers.

WAIS   Wide Area Information Server that allows you to search databases by keyword.

APPENDIX B
MASTER SITES RELATED TO GENERAL PSYCHOLOGY

The pages in this appendix describe a set of Web sites (on the Internet at the time of this writing) that we call "master sites" because they contain a tremendous amount of information regarding resources related to general psychology. The site descriptions are presented in alphabetical order.

For each site, the resources are listed in tabular form and divided into two parts. The first part of the table lets you know if information pertaining to academic research is available at the site. For instance, the checklist will give you information about whether databases, journal articles, or newsgroups can be accessed from that site. The second part of the table describes what information is available at the site to support psychology students in endeavors other than research, such as job hunting, career choices, and professional commitments.

Hopefully, these site descriptions will give you a quick overview of what each master site contains and will make it easier for you to get to the information you want. These sites are provided by reputable professional organizations, educational institutions, and commercial enterprises. Nevertheless, users are warned that no attempt has been made to evaluate the resources, and the authors cannot take responsibility for the accuracy of information at any site.

If you go to one of these sites and it suits your needs, we suggest that you bookmark it using your Web browser.

HOME PAGE: **American Psychological Association (PsychNet)**
URL ADDRESS: **http://www.apa.org**

Academic Research
___x___ Databases/archives
_____ Resources organized by psychology topics
___x___ Search tools
_____ Commercial software or shareware
_____ Newsgroups,discussions, or mailing lists
___x___ Electronic journals
_____ Resource persons
_____ Library catalogs
_____ Chat rooms
_____ Online tutorials and courses

Student Support for Psychology majors
_____ University/college/departments of psychology
___x___ Guides for writing using APA style
_____ Professional organizations
___x___ Conference information
___x___ Job opportunities
___x___ Self-help and mental health references
_____ Support groups/organizations
_____ Clinical and counseling services
___x___ Academic and career advisement

DESCRIPTION: **This Web site of the American Psychological Association presents public information about psychology and is a major reference for the professional psychologist and psychology students. Media releases, mental health brochures, and selected articles from the *APA Monitor* are some of its features. *PsychCrawler*, a new search engine located at this site, will search the indices of the APA and the National Institute of Mental Health (NIMH) Web sites**

HOME PAGE: **American Psychological Society**
URL ADDRESS: **http://psych.hanover.edu/APS**

Academic Research
___x___ Databases/archives
___x___ Resources organized by psychology topics
___x___ Search tools
___x___ Commercial software or shareware
_____ Newsgroups,discussions, or mailing lists
___x___ Electronic journals
_____ Resource persons
___x___ Library catalogs
_____ Chat rooms
_____ Online tutorials and courses

Student Support for Psychology majors
___x___ University/college/departments of psychology
___x___ Guides for writing using APA style
___x___ Professional organizations
_____ Conference information
___x___ Job opportunities
_____ Self-help and mental health references
_____ Support groups/organizations
_____ Clinical and counseling services
___x___ Academic and career advisement

DESCRIPTION: **The APS supports those interested in the scientific discipline of psychology. The site offers several Internet search tools, and has an index to electronic journals online. There are also many resources serving the needs of professionals in the field and students of psychology.**

HOME PAGE: **Cognitive and Psychological Sciences on the Internet**
URL ADDRESS: **http://matia.stanford.edu/cogsci/**

Academic Research
___x___ Databases/archives
___x___ Resources organized by psychology topics
_____ Search tools
___x___ Commercial software or shareware
___x___ Newsgroups,discussions, or mailing lists
___x___ Electronic journals
_____ Resource persons
_____ Library catalogs
_____ Chat rooms
_____ Online tutorials and courses

Student Support for Psychology majors
___x___ University/college/departments of psychology
___x___ Guides for writing using APA style
___x___ Professional organizations
___x___ Conference information
___x___ Job opportunities
_____ Self-help and mental health references
_____ Support groups/organizations
_____ Clinical and counseling services
___x___ Academic and career advisement

DESCRIPTION: **This is an index maintained by the Stanford
University Psychology Department and supported by the Virtual
Psychology Laboratory in England. Resources are relevant to
research in cognitive science and scientific psychology. The site has
several comprehensive lists of professional organizations, journals,
and discussions.**

66

HOME PAGE: **CyberPsychLink**
URL ADDRESS: **http://cctr.umkc.edu/user/dmartin/psych2.htm/**

Academic Research
__x__ Databases/archives
__x__ Resources organized by psychology topics
__x__ Search tools
__x__ Commercial software or shareware
__x__ Newsgroups,discussions, or mailing lists
__x__ Electronic journals
_____ Resource persons
__x__ Library catalogs
_____ Chat rooms
_____ Online tutorials and courses

Student Support for Psychology majors
_____ University/college/departments of psychology
__x__ Guides for writing using APA style
__x__ Professional organizations
__x__ Conference information
__x__ Job opportunities
__x__ Self-help and mental health references
__x__ Support groups/organizations
__x__ Clinical and counseling services
__x__ Academic and career advisement

DESCRIPTION: **This site is a good place to begin research on the Internet because there is such a variety of resources to choose from. Besides having links to several databases and archives of online publications, there are links to library catalogs which you can use to search for printed publications. The links to mailing lists and newsgroups will help you find discussions of a number of topics. The site also has a wealth of support resources for students.**

HOME PAGE: **Hanover College Psychology Department**
URL ADDRESS: **http://psych.hanover.edu/**

Academic Research
___x___ Databases/archives
_____ Resources organized by psychology topics
___x___ Search tools
___x___ Commercial software or shareware
_____ Newsgroups,discussions, or mailing lists
___x___ Electronic journals
_____ Resource persons
___x___ Library catalogs
_____ Chat rooms
___x___ Online tutorials and courses

Student Support for Psychology majors
___x___ University/college/departments of psychology
___x___ Guides for writing using APA style
___x___ Professional organizations
_____ Conference information
___x___ Job opportunities
___x___ Self-help and mental health references
_____ Support groups/organizations
_____ Clinical and counseling services
___x___ Academic and career advisement

DESCRIPTION: **Hanover College's page is designed for their psychology majors. However, the site is valuable to anyone wanting to get to a large number of psychology-related Internet resources in an efficient manner. Resources are clearly organized into categories and the "miscellaneous psychology links" category lists resources in alphabetical order.**

HOME PAGE: **The Psychology Jumping Stand**
URL ADDRESS: **http://www.indiana.edu:80/~iuepsyc/Psyc/Jump.html**

Academic Research
__x__ Databases/archives
__x__ Resources organized by psychology topics
_____ Search tools
_____ Commercial software or shareware
_____ Newsgroups,discussions, or mailing lists
__x__ Electronic journals
_____ Resource persons
_____ Library catalogs
_____ Chat rooms
__x__ Online tutorials and courses

Student Support for Psychology majors
_____ University/college/departments of psychology
__x__ Guides for writing using APA style
__x__ Professional organizations
__x__ Conference information
__x__ Job opportunities
_____ Self-help and mental health references
_____ Support groups/organizations
_____ Clinical and counseling services
__x__ Academic and career advisement

DESCRIPTION: **This site has lots of student support resources, including APA Style FAQs, a "how to study" guide, and help on effective presentations. Resources are organized by topics usually found in an Introductory Psychology textbook. There are links to several tutorials and exercises, journal articles, and excerpts from books.**

HOME PAGE: **PsychREF**
URL ADDRESS: **http://maple.lemoyne.edu/~hevern/psychref2.html**

Academic Research

- x   Databases/archives
- x   Resources organized by psychology topics
- x   Search tools
- x   Commercial software or shareware
- x   Newsgroups,discussions, or mailing lists
- x   Electronic journals
-     Resource persons
-     Library catalogs
-     Chat rooms
- x   Online tutorials and courses

Student Support for Psychology majors

-     University/college/departments of psychology
- x   Guides for writing using APA style
- x   Professional organizations
- x   Conference information
-     Job opportunities
-     Self-help and mental health references
-     Support groups/organizations
-     Clinical and counseling services
- x   Academic and career advisement

DESCRIPTION: **The site is designed for undergraduate psychology students and faculty, especially those who are doing research. Resources are organized by academic topic, and there are quite an extensive number of resources related to ethical issues in research and practice. Students will find many resources related to writing reports and using APA style.**

70

HOME PAGE: **Psych Web**
URL ADDRESS: **http://www.psych-web.com/index.html**

Academic Research
__x__ Databases/archives
__x__ Resources organized by psychology topics
__x__ Search tools
__x__ Commercial software or shareware
__x__ Newsgroups,discussions, or mailing lists
__x__ Electronic journals
_____ Resource persons
_____ Library catalogs
_____ Chat rooms
__x__ Online tutorials and courses

Student Support for Psychology majors
__x__ University/college/departments of psychology
__x__ Guides for writing using APA style
__x__ Professional organizations
__x__ Conference information
__x__ Job opportunities
__x__ Self-help and mental health references
__x__ Support groups/organizations
__x__ Clinical and counseling services
__x__ Academic and career advisement

DESCRIPTION: **Psych Web is especially suited for psychology students with many "tip sheets" on careers and graduate study in psychology. There is a very comprehensive listing of resources categorized by topic and separated into scholarly and self-help categories. You can reach the popular "Mind Tools" from this site, as well.**

HOME PAGE: **PsycSite**
URL ADDRESS: **http://stange.simplenet.com/psycsite/**

Academic Research
  x   Databases/archives
  x   Resources organized by psychology topics
  x   Search tools
  x   Commercial software or shareware
  x   Newsgroups, discussions, or mailing lists
  x   Electronic journals
  x   Resource persons
      Library catalogs
  x   Chat rooms
  x   Online tutorials and courses

Student Support for Psychology majors
  x   University/college/departments of psychology
  x   Guides for writing using APA style
  x   Professional organizations
  x   Conference information
  x   Job opportunities
      Self-help and mental health references
      Support groups/organizations
      Clinical and counseling services
  x   Academic and career advisement

DESCRIPTION: **This Canadian site is one of the best master sites available for resources that focus on the science of psychology. Net sites that involve self-help or parapsychology are excluded from the listings at this site. There are an extensive number of pointers to journals, abstracts, and databases, and they are organized by topic. Some links lead to full-text scholarly articles published online.**